Sophie ♡ ♡ ♡
You are most exceptional when you are your funny, fiesty, fabulous self! Don't ever lose your sparkle!!!

We are so proud of you ♡ xxxxx
Love Always,
Uncle Harry
& Aunty Alexa

Most Exceptional ME

by Tiffany Malas & Lauren Maerz

Illustrated by Dan McGeehan

PROLANCE

"Sam, time to wake up. You have school today," my mommy says in a loving way.

We pack my bag and head to the car.
I have my favorite lunchbox. The one with a star.

She walks me to class and kisses me goodbye.
I'm a big kid now so there's no reason to cry.

I go inside and put my things in my cubby.
Then go to the circle and sit by my buddy.
Ms. G asks us,
"What's the date today?"
I raise my hand because
I know what to say.

In a proud voice I answer, "It's the first day of September!"

But I was wrong. Ugh! Why couldn't I remember?

My face turns red. My body feels tight.
"You're most exceptional,"
Ms. G says when
I don't get it right.

Ms. G traces the fingers on her hand.
One deep breath in, out at the top, I understand.

I do this five times. What a difference it makes!
I feel ready again. Sometimes I just need to take breaks.

So I look at the calendar
and then try once more.

I got it!

I say,

"It's
September
24!"

It's time to move on so I go get my book.
Back at the circle I read the word "look."

But the words get harder.
I'm reading them wrong.
If I don't get this right,
I'll be here too long!

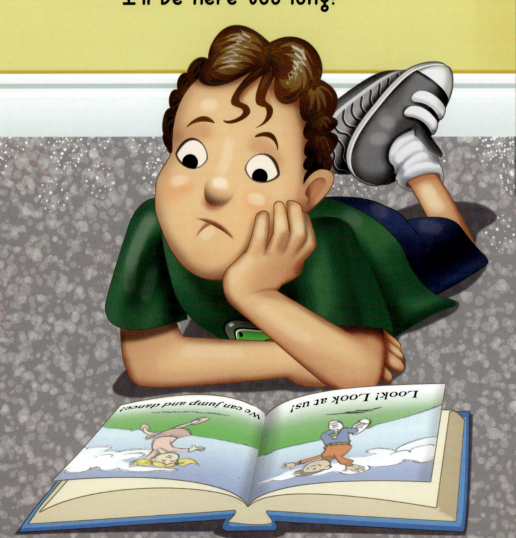

When I start to feel tears fall down my face,
Ms. G comes to join me in my space.

"You're most exceptional," she says,
"there's no need to cry."

So I take some deep breaths
and give it a try.

I make the sound of every letter.
My reading is getting so much better!

I did it!

I read all the words in my book!
Blending the sounds is all that it took.

I go back to my desk with a smirk
and when I sit down, I'm ready to work.

1+1=2, 3+1=4

I can do it!
I'm ready for more!

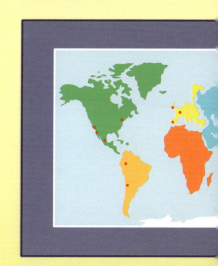

6+1=7, 8+1=10?
Uh-oh, I have that bad feeling again.
"This is too hard," I tell Ms. G.
"I don't know how!"
She says,
"You're most
 exceptional, Sam!
You can't quit now."

I count eight blocks and add the next one.
I raise my hand so Ms. G knows I'm done.
She gives me a high five for how hard I've tried.
I'm starting to feel so much better inside.
A big smile comes over my face.
I just had to take my time.
Learning is not a race.

I put my things away and get ready to go home.
Then I wait for my friend so I don't walk alone.
He drops his sticker as he walks to the bus.
The one for doing our work that Ms. G gave to us.

I think about keeping it. It's really cool!
But then his mommy won't know how well he did in school.

"Wait! You dropped your sticker," I quickly say.
"Oh, thanks Sam," he says in a happy way.
It's nice to make others feel good too.
Helping is something I like to do.

In the car my mommy asks,
"How was
     school today?"
Where do I begin? There is so much to say!
I think about my hard but exceptional day
and how I calmed myself down with Ms. G's special way.

"Today I learned how to read and add.
If I make a mistake, it's not that bad.
All I need to do is take my time
   and if I don't give up, I'll be just fine.
      But best of all I learned that
         I am most exceptional,

M.E.,
and there is
no one else
in the world
I would
rather be!"

About the authors:

Tiffany and Lauren met in 2012 during their graduate studies in Communication Disorders. Tiffany later completed her masters at Chapman University and Lauren completed hers at San Diego State University. They both pursued careers as Speech-Language Pathologists working with children in elementary school and private practice settings.

It wasn't until they began working in the field that they realized the tremendous role emotional well-being plays in a child's academic and social success. This inspired them to come together to create Most Exceptional ME as a resource for children, parents, teachers, and therapists. It is their hope that Sam will inspire children to work through uncomfortable emotions by identifying their feelings and believing in themselves. After all, when confidence and creativity are encouraged, a child is capable of anything.

About the illustrator:

Dan McGeehan wears many different hats. He is an illustrator, an actor, a director, and a playwright. His whimsical, colorful illustrations have appeared in a wide range of magazines, advertisements, and children's books for over forty years. Additionally, he has participated in or directed over two hundred performances all around the country including plays, ballets, and even movies. And he is also the author of several plays that have been performed in countries all around the world.

For FREE **Most Exceptional ME** resources
please visit www.prolancewriting.com/most-exceptional-me

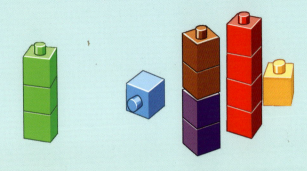